Healthy Me

I
Love
Fruit

I
Love
Veggies

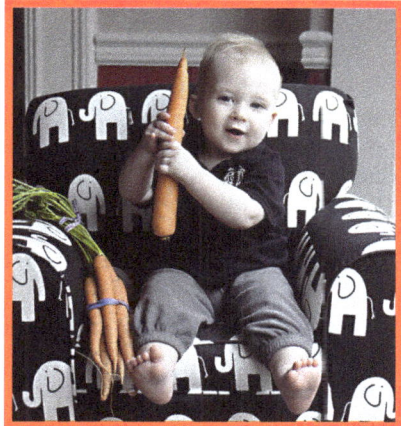

Written and Illustrated by
Klaus Bohn

CCB Publishing, British Columbia, Canada

Healthy Me: I Love Fruit, I Love Veggies

Copyright ©2012 by Klaus Bohn
ISBN-13   978-1-77143-034-0
First Edition

Library and Archives Canada Cataloguing in Publication
Bohn, Klaus
Healthy me : I love fruit, I love veggies /
written and illustrated by Klaus Bohn.
ISBN 978-1-77143-034-0
Also issued in electronic format.
Additional cataloguing data available from Library and Archives Canada

Publisher: CCB Publishing
                British Columbia, Canada
                www.ccbpublishing.com

This book is dedicated to my grandchildren...

Pippa

and

Charlie

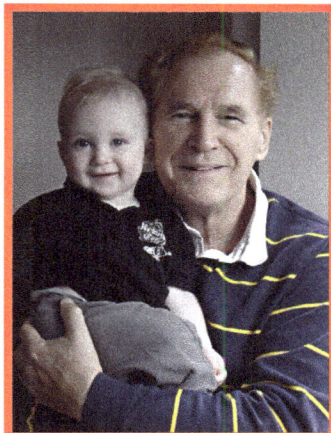

My pride and joy...

Love loves to please

Special thanks to their loving Uncle David, my middle child, for his help in designing the cover.

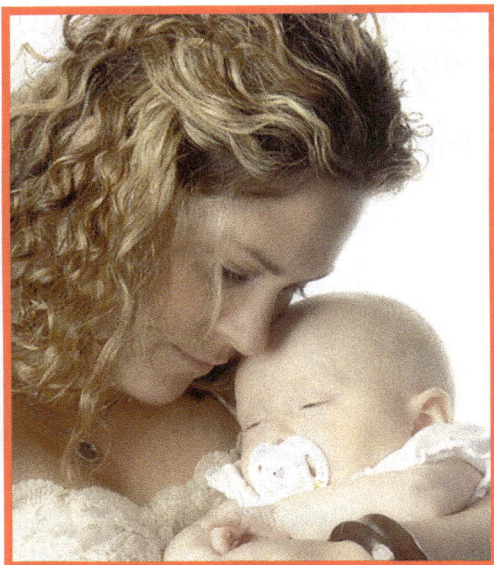

My daughter Tammy is Pippa's mother.

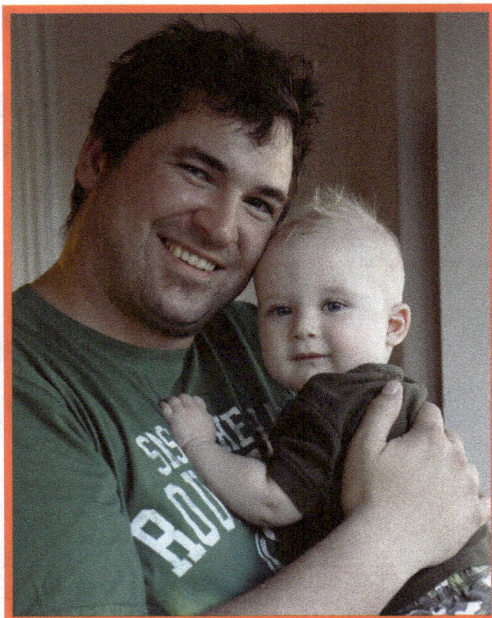

My son Michael is Charlie's father.

Fruits and
vegetables are
natural foods
for the body
to stay healthy
all your life.
It is great to
enjoy what
you eat.

Bananas

Green Apples

Lemons

Oranges

Pumpkins

Watermelons

Apples

Pomegranates

Red Peppers

Yellow Peppers

Fruit
trees
in
the
yard
yumeee

Life is full of
imagination
and
daydreams.

May we keep
our childlike
fun with us
always.

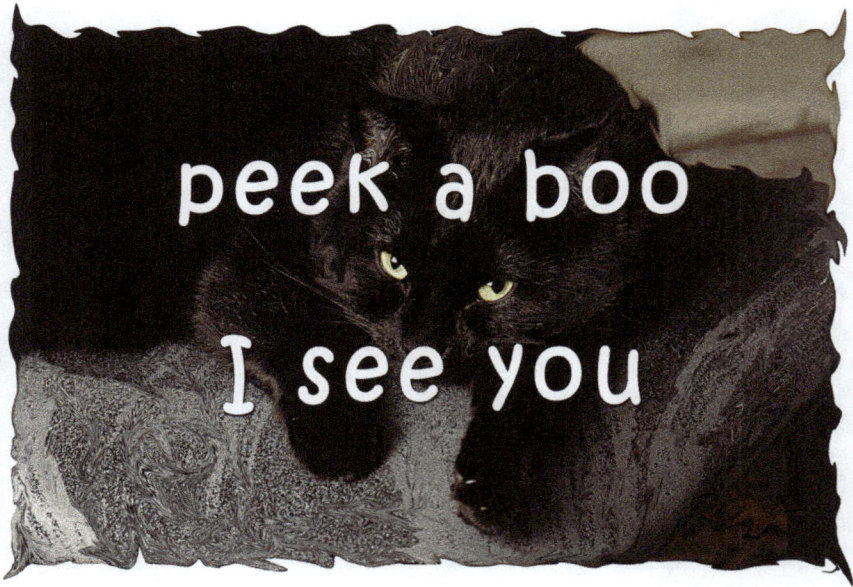

peek a boo

I see you

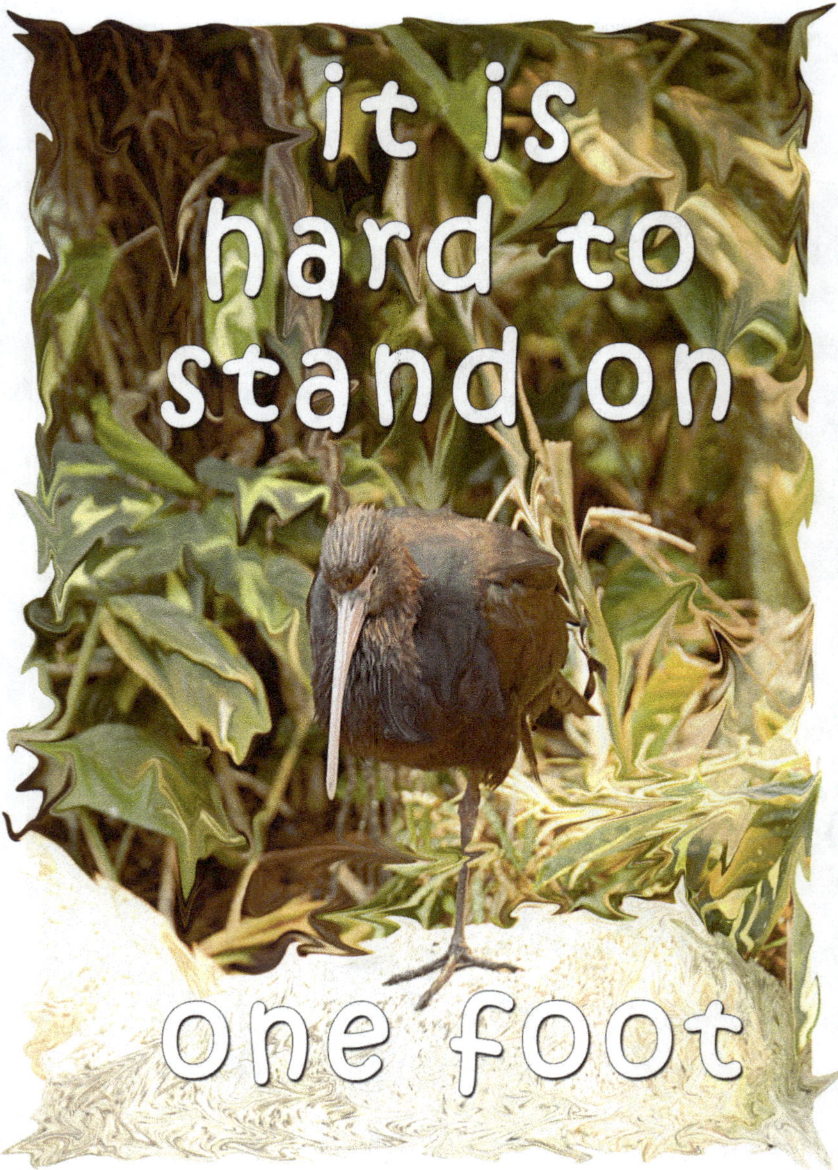

it is hard to stand on one foot

I love to just
hang around

14

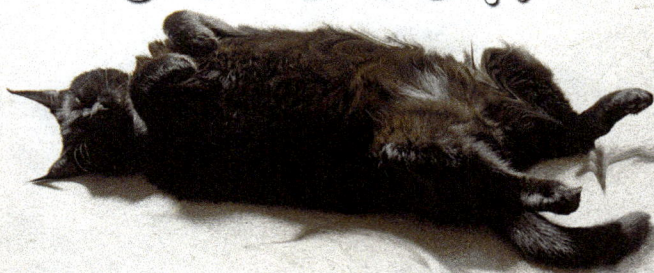

stretch

love the
garden
to see
and enjoy

18

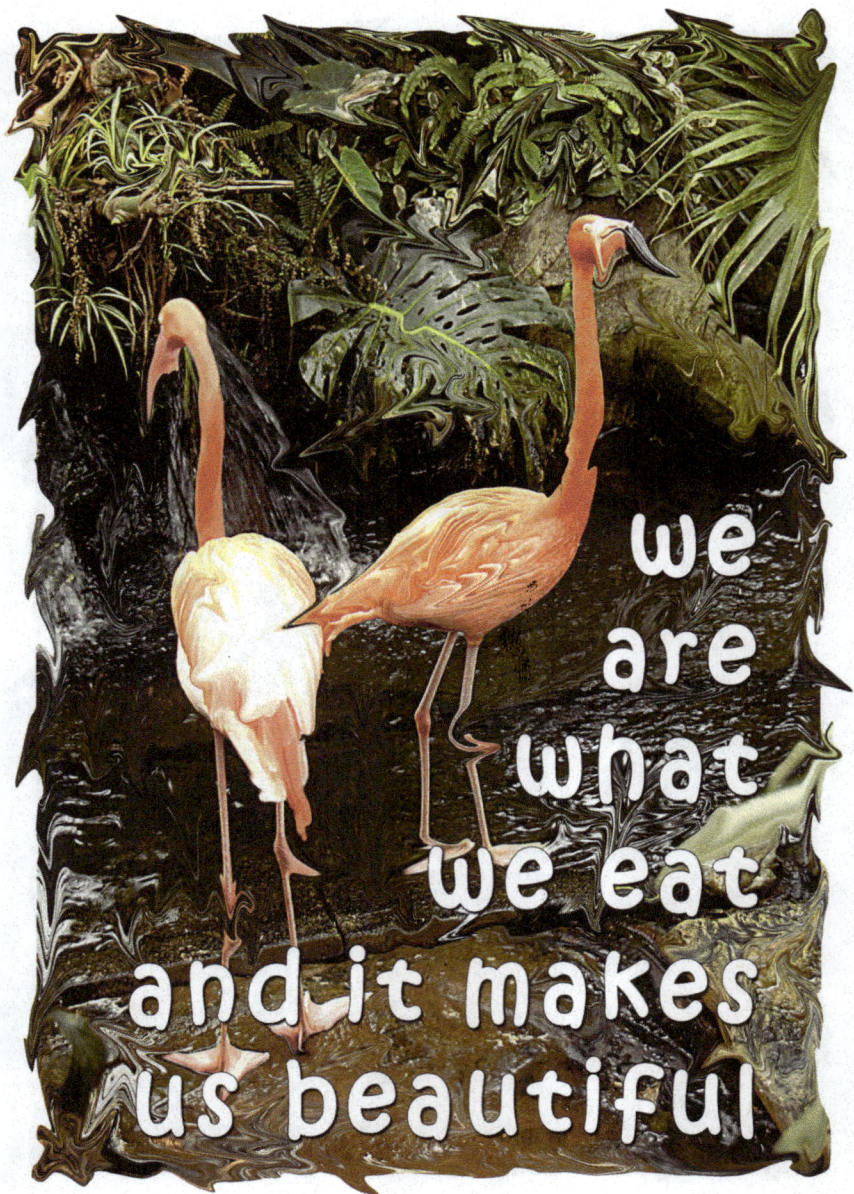

we
are
what
we eat
and it makes
us beautiful

sweet
to
smell
hummm

hummingbirds
enjoy
friendship

be my friend

kites flying
together
like friends

beautiful
lily

28

climbing
lizard

parrots
love to look

love to
drink
water
because
it is healthy

elephants
are
wise
with
age

As we grow
in years may we
become wise.

Maturity comes
with age.

sad faced onion
because it makes
my eyes water

38

About the Author/Illustrator

For over thirty years Klaus Bohn has worked to develop his unique style and received his Fellowship (F/SPPA) and Craftsman (CPA) in 1987 and his Masters of Photographic Arts (MPA) in 1989. He has also received his Accreditation in Child Photography along with many other awards for Excellence in Photography.

His insights, gained from decades of discovery, are shared to assist all photographers capture more creative and vibrant images. You too will be *feeling more deeply about photography*, which is Klaus Bohn's brand.

To find out more about Klaus, his work and his other books (see back cover), please visit his web sites:

www.photographicartvictoria.com

www.photographicartbyklausbohn.com

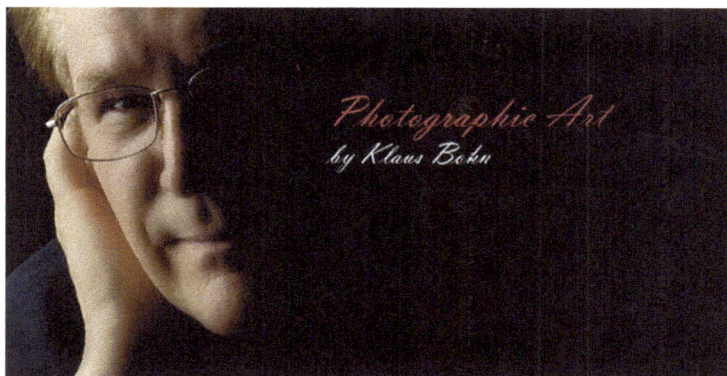

Photographic Art
by Klaus Bohn